D1563265

A Perfect Wedding

Eric & Leslie Ludy

HARVEST HOUSE PUBLISHERS

EUGENE, OREGON

Eric Ludy: Published in association with Loyal Arts Literary Agency, LoyalArts.com.

Leslie Ludy: Published in association with Loyal Arts Literary Agency, LoyalArts.com.

Cover by Koechel Peterson & Associates, Inc., Minneapolis, Minnesota

Cover photo © Ingram Publishing/Matton Images

A PERFECT WEDDING
Copyright © 2006 by Winston and Brooks, Inc.
Published by Harvest House Publishers
Eugene, Oregon 97402
www.harvesthousepublishers.com

Library of Congress Cataloging-in-Publication Data

Ludy, Eric.
  A perfect wedding / Eric and Leslie Ludy.
          p. cm.
    ISBN-13: 978-0-7369-1566-3 (pbk.)
    ISBN-10: 0-7369-1566-4
  1. Marriage—Religious aspects—Christianity.   2. Weddings.   I. Ludy,
Leslie.   II. Title.
    BV835.L825 2006
    265'.5—dc22   2005020895

Printed in China

          06 07 08 09 10 11 12 13 14 /IM-CF / 10 9 8 7 6 5 4 3 2 1

Contents

꙰꙰꙰

Whatever Happened to "Happily Ever After"?

When we reach our graying years and
we gaze back upon our life, we will look
at our wedding day, perhaps more than
any other, as either the start of something
great or the start of something grating.

So, Eric, we hear you and Leslie are getting married—
that's great! Congratulations! Just make sure you soak
up the romance while you can—because once the honeymoon is
over...it's really over!"

From the day Leslie and I announced our engagement, we were

showered with congratulations, best wishes...and wet blankets. Plenty of well-meaning people did their best to prepare us for the "dismal reality" of marriage. We heard enough tales about stale romance, annoying habits, and insensitive marriage partners to last us well beyond our golden anniversary.

Whatever happened to "happily ever after"?

It's been about ten thousand years now since Adam and Eve first tied the knot and then launched the marriage industry with an unceremonious market crash. That very first marriage didn't get off on the best footing with that snake and apple and all. Add to that the eviction notice that soon followed, and you'd have to wonder where the concept of "happily ever after" really came from.

Marriage has had bad publicity from the very start.

The marriage business has a lot of extremely dissatisfied customers. Very few married folk (or previously married folk) have glowing reviews about their stints as husband and wife. Most would tell you that the excitement they experienced during their honeymoon eroded hastily into a stale relationship marked by bickering and ever-growing resentment as the months and years passed.

The romance tanks, the sex dries up, he doesn't listen, she is a constant nag—the whole beautiful experience somehow loses its luster. Husbands grumble and wives have nightly headaches, but they stick it out for eighteen more years "for the sake of the kids." This is the sickening reality of a majority of modern marriages—a sad soap opera of disillusionment and pain.

Not much of a sales pitch, is it?

Amazingly, we of the marrying age have spent a lifetime getting an earful of this bad publicity, and yet we still desire to stand with our true love and declare "I do" in front of a church full of witnesses. We've heard the cynics' complaints ad nauseum, we've witnessed marital trauma up close...and yet we still long to toss the bouquet and remove the garter.

Why?

Are we idiots? Emotionally blinded optimists? Self-defeating masochists? A mixture of all three?

In spite of all the bad press marriage gets, something within us wants to prove that the divorce epidemic won't strike *our* home. We believe that we can live differently from all those who failed. We believe that we can figure out the secret to a lasting love story. We believe that marriage, *if done right,* is worth the outrageously huge risk of it all falling apart if it's not.

Marriage fascinates us—it woos us with its shimmer of possible beauty and the hope that we will ride off into the sunset for a lifetime of satisfaction. Marriage has woven into its fabric the gold thread of something heavenly...if only we can figure it out and make it all work.

So despite the awful reviews by the multitudes of dissatisfied marriage customers, we press on, we propose, we set the date, we send out the invitations, we register, we book the church, we anticipate the day, we exchange the vows, we exchange the rings, we kiss at the altar...*and we hope.*

We hope that what we possess as a couple is a stronger variety of love than that which the millions of failed marriages before us possessed.

Those of us who refuse to surrender to the prophecy of marriage mediocrity—what will we find in the end? Will we find that taste of heaven on earth that we so desperately long for? Will we find the "happily ever after" romance we've always dreamed of?

Our success depends on the foundation we lay *now—before* we walk down the aisle. Just as the success of a farmer's crop is determined long before the harvest time arrives, so the ultimate success of our marriage depends on the seeds we choose to plant in the springtime season of our relationship.

Beautiful lifelong romance *is* possible. God's design is for a couple to thrive and grow in their love and intimacy throughout their lifetime. But these kinds of love stories are rare because the pattern by which they are built has fallen into obscurity.

In this little book, our desire is to dust off God's ancient path—a path that leads couples to the perfection of marriage intimacy. The answer is not roses, rhymes, tender rhetoric, or even raw grit and determination. Rather, the Author of romance Himself wants to be your Wedding Planner.

A wedding day doesn't define a great and lasting marriage, but like a pulse, it identifies the life at the center of it. Humanly built wedding days set up couples for humanly marred marriages, but God-crafted wedding days provide a foundation for a beautiful lifetime of profound shared intimacy.

A wedding day is a taste of what's to come. The tenor of a wedding day can often be the tenor of an entire marriage. Is a wedding about *you*, the bride and groom, or is it about Someone *greater than you?* Those who learn to answer this all-important question correctly unlock the great mystery of marital success. The way we approach our wedding day gives great insight into the way we'll approach all the rest of the days of our life.

If you are like the many other couples in our generation who long for something more than mediocrity in your future marriage, then get off to the right start by assigning God the position of Wedding Coordinator. Allow Him to teach you what a wedding day is really meant to be about.

God loves wedding days. He designed them to be a picture of heaven on earth. He invented them to be a foretaste of something far bigger than bride and groom, far more than the cake and flowers. *He created weddings to be a demonstration of who He is.*

So allow God to show you how breathtakingly beautiful your wedding day can be when the Author of lasting love becomes the Guest of Honor.

CHAPTER ONE

A Poetic Love

Beyond Roses and Rhymes

Experience the matchless beauty
of faithfulness for a lifetime.

To love a spouse amid the flame of honeymoon
passion is human, but to love a spouse all the
days of your life, even before you ever lay eyes
upon that person—this kind of love is divine.

op-culture love certainly has its appeal. To be a real-life character in *Sex and the City* or on the sitcom *Friends* would have been the ultimate dream for many. It's a devil-may-care lifestyle, red hot with passion and loaded with all sorts of fantastic, exhilarating sensations.

But at its core is selfishness.

Pop-culture love craves sexual fulfillment at the expense of every other virtue—even at the expense of having a real relationship that actually works.

Selfishness and lifelong romance are like oil and water; they naturally separate when thrown together. And most modern couples find out too late that *pop-culture love doesn't work in marriage.* It's like trying to run a car engine on a fifth of vodka— it will burp, snort, and bang to a halt only a few miles down the interstate of life.

When God becomes our Wedding Coordinator, the first thing He scraps is the notion of selfish love. He is into *forever* relationships, not five-hour flings. His goal is not only to make our relationship work but to make it thrive romantically for a lifetime. To do that, He must introduce us to a far superior version of love. God's version of love is not trumpeted by modern media outlets or heralded in the saucy self-help magazine articles of our day. This superior version of love is God's select brand from His own personal stock. All the money in the world cannot purchase it, but He offers it freely to those who simply ask.

But there is one catch. We can't have God's love and maintain a pop-culture lifestyle of selfishness. Selfish love and God's *self-less* love can't coexist—which means things have to change in our lives when God's love enters the picture. The theme of our lives can no longer be about what *we* want; it has to be about what God wants and about what is best for those around us.

Selfish love comes naturally to us—we don't have to labor to be excellent at it. But God's love on the other hand is opposite our bent. We have to allow our lives to be *remade* to exhibit its glory.

A Poetic Love

For most, the highest ideals of love bring to mind moonlit serenades, dozens of roses, and ardent rhymes that troll the depths of a lover's feelings. These pictures of romance are wonderful, but they barely scratch the surface of what is possible with God's version of love.

God invented marriage, romance, and sexuality, so wouldn't He naturally know best how we can maximize these things in our lives?

God designed the beauty of romance to stretch through an entire life, not to sputter its final breath after the honeymoon ends. God's version of love goes the distance—He's a fan of things that last forever. And to help us in such a forever kind of endeavor, He offers us a version of love that can withstand the harshest winds of time. It's not a pop-culture love but *a poetic love*—so fabulously beautiful that it is nearly impossible to describe.

A poetic love is a *selfless* love. It's noble, it's pure, it's tender, it's dignified, it's grand...*it's heavenly.* We all have our moments of selfless nobility, but poetic love isn't a one-time heroic deed. Rather, it's a lifelong lifestyle of romantic service to our spouse.

Poetic love is made up of three magnificent ingredients that we can blend together consistently in a marriage relationship to create a "heaven on earth" experience. Let's look closer at these three ingredients that are capable of launching our marriages into the stratosphere of divine beauty.

Lifelong Thoughtfulness

Thoughtfulness is the catalyst to romance. Without it, a relationship is flavorless and one-dimensional. Many couples practice thoughtfulness while they are falling in love. They write poetry, sing love songs, buy flowers, and express their affections by doing a thousand crazy things that only someone in love would do.

Falling in love is a fun and amazing experience, but very few of us realize that the thrill of thoughtfulness for a spouse was never meant to be isolated merely to the falling-in-love season of a relationship. In fact, most couples today completely miss two far more significant times to practice thoughtfulness in a relationship.

First, God intended thoughtfulness to be *lifelong*. That means lovers should put it into practice even *before* they ever meet, and then it can be the catalyst to romantic beauty throughout married life. The secret to God's poetic love is that it is proactive and persevering. It goes into action long before the first hello is exchanged. And it continues through sickness and health, for richer and for poorer.

Imagine what you could do for your marriage if, before you ever met your spouse, you were thoughtful toward that person. And because you cared for your future spouse so much, you set your life aside just for that person...heart, mind, and body.

Imagine if from a young age you had served your future spouse, prayed for him or her, written love letters and love songs for that person alone, and shooed away everyone else who vied for that sacred position in your life.

What if you wrote your spouse love letters long before you ever knew his or her name? Imagine what an amazing gift you could give your spouse on your wedding day.

This is Christ's model for loving a spouse. His love for us is proactive. Jesus died on the cross for each of us and dealt with the penalty of our sin long before we personally needed it. And this is the model He desires to teach us for our wedding day and for all the years of romance that will follow.

Even if you haven't been practicing this kind of proactive and poetic love before now, *start today*. Start investing in your marriage now, before you walk down that aisle.

God intends you to marry only one person, so begin living as if only one person will ever have access to your heart. That's God's way.

Sexual Devotion

If you are thoughtful toward your spouse throughout your lifetime, then of course you will also be sexually set apart just for him or her.

A white dress is an outward symbol of a bride's inward purity. A wedding day, as God originally intended it, is a celebration of two young people who have faithfully waited their entire lifetimes just for each other, to bond together and finally enjoy the rewards of their patience.

Sexual devotion is not just a bonus blessing in a marriage. It is a foundation for God's forever kind of love. God created a proper context for the exploration of sexual intimacy, and when that context is kept sacred, a couple discovers an amazing depth of satisfaction in each other and quickly understands why God says to wait.

What if you have violated this sacred boundary? Hope is not lost—you can experience God's wonderful gift of restoration, but you must allow Him to take you through a rebuilding season. Let Him refocus and reestablish the foundation stones of success at the core of your romantic relationship. Let Him wash you clean and give you a fresh start. God is in the business of offering beautiful new beginnings.

Make the decision to love your spouse by being sexually set apart for him or her from this day forward. Jealously protect every expression of physical intimacy as a sacred treasure for your lifetime lover. Sexual allurement is seemingly all around us in today's world. But instead of treating it casually, give your spouse the gift of faithfulness by guarding your heart, eyes, and mind from the temptations of the culture. Let your desire be for your spouse alone, and you will discover the fullness, freedom, and beauty of God-centered sexual intimacy.

Outrageous Generosity

To sexually set your life apart for your spouse out of duty is one thing. But God desires you to be sexually set apart for your spouse not from a sense of obligation but as an outflow of selfless and purposeful love.

We could easily complain about this whole purity thing and bemoan the fact that people without convictions seem to have all the fun. But that attitude only breeds discontent and offers no benefit to your future.

When God plans a wedding day, two people set their lives aside for one another willingly and with great enthusiasm, knowing that every challenge and difficulty in doing so only serves to strengthen their future marriage relationship. God never wastes a test of patience.

The final piece of God's poetic love is outrageous generosity. God wants to build lovers who love as He does—with abandon. They give everything, with all their heart, soul, mind, and strength. They sacrifice and face the most challenging difficulties for the "joy set before them" (see Hebrews 12:2).

Before you get married, learn to give *everything*—and learn to give as if giving were the greatest pleasure, because it is. Learn to stop figuring what *you* should be getting out of the deal. Learn to give without a required payback. Learn to give simply because God has given so much to you.

A poetic love is rare these days, but it is not out of reach. It will cost you everything, but what you receive in return is worth more than everything you possess now and everything you could possess for a thousand lifetimes.

Remember, God doesn't need to imitate our culture's style of love and romance. God has His own version of love—a poetic love that far surpasses anything Hollywood could ever create.

A wedding day marked by poetic love is a wedding day that evidences the nature of God Himself—the original Author of true and lasting love.

PUTTING A POETIC LOVE INTO ACTION ON YOUR WEDDING DAY

A Foot-Washing Ceremony

When Christ was here on earth, He made an incredible statement of His selfless love for His bride when He removed His outer garment, wrapped a towel around His waist, and washed His disciples' feet (John 13:1-5). By this act, He was declaring to His bride, "I will love you selflessly. I will serve you with all I am and all I have. I will lay down My life for you." The world has never seen a greater demonstration of poetic love than Christ's sacrificial, outrageous love for His bride. Though we are so unworthy, the King of the universe stoops to gently wash our feet.

On your wedding day, make this same declaration to your spouse by tenderly washing each other's feet as a symbol of your commitment to serve each other selflessly for a lifetime. You might choose to have an actual foot-washing ceremony as part of your wedding, as Leslie and I did. Or you might choose to wash each other's feet in a different way. For example, you could write letters to each other, stating your commitment to pour out your life in selfless service for the other person. Then frame the letters and display them in an important place as a reminder of your decision. Whatever way you choose to wash your lover's feet, the important thing is to declare your commitment to selflessly serve your spouse and, even more importantly, to live out that commitment on a day-to-day basis.

Faithfully

We originally wrote this song as an accompaniment to our book *When God Writes Your Love Story*. We wrote it to capture the inexpressible beauty of a poetic love—setting your life aside for one person for a lifetime. We've received many letters and e-mails over the years from people who have used this song in their wedding ceremony. This inspired us to finally write the following version of the song...especially for a God-scripted wedding day.

Tonight I saw a shooting star
Reminded me of everything you are
All my life I dreamed of you
And wondered if I'd see my dreams come true

In this world of cheap romance
And love that only fades after the dance
They said I was a fool to wait for something more
But when I look into your eyes, it's all I've waited for
You'll never know just what you mean to me
For as long as I live I'll love you faithfully

CHORUS
Faithfully I am yours
From now until forever
Faithfully I will write
Write you a love song with my life
'Cause this kind of love's worth waiting for
Until the end of all time
I am yours faithfully

Tonight I seal my promise with this kiss
Whatever lies ahead, remember this
My heart has always been yours alone
And I belong to you from this day on

In this world of broken dreams
And promises that never seem to keep
They might say we're fools to live for something more
But you are part of who I am,
You're etched upon my soul
The years won't change all that you are to me
For a lifetime and a day I'll love you faithfully

CHAPTER TWO

A Sacred Vow

Beyond the Words "I Do"

*Exchange all: Share a holy covenant
where two become one.*

*To give up everything for all time...this
is not a decision to make with haste.*

*L*eslie and I love to do little romantic things for each other. We strategically leave love notes in odd locations, share tender kisses secretly in unexpected moments, sing love songs with sincere though sometimes warbled affection, and give a hundred other creative expressions that say the same thing over and over and over again: "You are my chosen one!"

The two of us never bore of these little utterances of love. The love notes don't need to wax poetic, the roses don't have to be fresh, and the kisses don't have to be moist. The utterances can be imperfect because the message behind them all is unblemished and utterly perfect. Each of these romantic gestures in its own way expresses the foundation of what makes marriage so great. These acts continually remind us that we have chosen each other for a lifetime.

Marriage offers the context to fully enjoy the beauty of such expressions. Sure, these same things are wonderful before marriage when you are falling in love, but after the wedding they carry an entirely new dimension of meaning. Why? Because they are backed by a commitment for all time—they are backed by *covenant,* a life-altering and forever binding decision.

A couple in a steamy physical romance could never cultivate the same depth of connection Leslie and I share in our marriage without first entering into a covenant relationship with each other.

You can't entrust yourself to someone fully without a commitment that spans good times and bad times. You can't hear the authentic ring of true devotion in a love song with no foundation of complete and utter trust. A covenant establishes a dauntless confidence from which to enjoy your spouse and soak up the thrill of life together.

A covenant is not a contract. It's not a business agreement scrawled on a piece of notebook paper that either party can terminate on a disgruntled whim. It's not a "feel good" transaction designed to get a whole bunch of free wedding gifts. A marriage covenant is an ancient ceremony, a solemn act, a sacred vow. It's a binding of two lives, the forging of two destinies for a common purpose. It is the most holy, most sacred, most celebrated, and most serious act a human being can make. A marriage covenant defines your life, your behavior, and all your future decisions from the moment you say "I do." It is the central and cardinal reason for a wedding day.

The covenant is what ties a love relationship together. It's what gives kisses sparkle, love notes meaning, and love songs depth.

If Leslie and I hadn't formed our marriage covenant, we wouldn't be where we are today, intimately sharing in each other's lives. Sure, we might be able to have a shallow, physical romance, but we would have no authentic, lifelong, always-growing love story. To access the depths of who Leslie is, and to gain the affectionate intimacy we now share together as a couple, I needed to enter into a sacred covenant with her. I had to make her my chosen one.

A wedding day designed by God focuses all its energies into the transaction of the covenant. All the pomp and circumstance surrounding a wedding serve to accentuate the significance of the solemn and momentous binding of two lives as one. A wedding isn't about the dress or the tux, the stringed quartet, the flowers, the candelabras, the gifts, the rings, or even the bride or the groom. *It's about the covenant exchange and the God who oversees it.*

In God's economy, a wedding covenant is an earthly picture of a much more significant covenant that He established with His bride nearly two thousand years ago. And God intends every wedding to be a reminder of that blood covenant, which He invites each and every one of us to enter into with Him.

A marriage covenant is the offering of my entire person to another, to love her and serve her...*for all time.* It means surrendering my single self-directed life for a shared life as one. It means releasing my grip on all my possessions, allowing them to no longer be mine but ours. It means giving up the freedom I once enjoyed to give my love to anyone, for the commitment to give my love to only one for the rest of my life. It means never again thinking things through from my perspective alone, but from this point forward, adopting my spouse's perspective as a primary guideline for all the many decisions life brings. It means surrendering my old identity and taking on a new name. It means leaving my self-satisfying life as I once knew it for a life of service to my spouse. I am no longer my own—I have given my life away. And it's important to note that I can never take it back.

Covenant making is serious business. God treats covenants as binding and forever. When He covenants with us, He doesn't ever change His mind. He Himself is bound by covenant. He gives Himself entirely to us, everything He is and everything He has—*His entire life.* His only request is that we give ourselves entirely to Him in return. That's the gospel...it's an invitation to enter a covenant with the God of the universe, to become one with Him and to enjoy the fullness of His person for eternity.

And that's the essence of a wedding day—offering our entire life unequivocally to another, to become one with them and enjoy the fullness of their person for a lifetime.

Sure, it can be a little scary when we begin to understand covenant through God's eyes, but a bit of squirming is good for us. A little trepidation forces us to think things through on a higher and deeper level, and it works to purify our intentions and our expectations as we approach our wedding day. But oh, how beautiful a covenant is when we understand the gravity of it and yet still choose to give our all...for all time.

Someone in love wants more than just kisses, love notes, and love songs for a lifetime. After a while the sparkle of each of those fabulous things will begin to fade if it is not backed up by a covenant commitment. The sacred vow of covenant, the sacred "I do," is what brings out the unprecedented beauty of romance in a marriage. Your spouse doesn't just want to be fawned over; he or she desires to be your chosen one. Your spouse desires an irrevocable covenant commitment.

The same is true with our King. He is eager for us to obey His truth, write Him love notes, and sing Him love songs, but as our chosen King, He desires a binding, non-retractable covenant commitment from us. He desires to enter into a holy exchange with us. He wants us to trade our self-made life for His divine life within us.

PUTTING A SACRED VOW INTO ACTION ON YOUR WEDDING DAY

Communion

On the night of Christ's crucifixion, He entered into a covenant relationship with His bride by breaking bread and drinking wine with His disciples at the last supper. The broken bread symbolized His body, broken on our behalf—His sacrificial choice to give everything for us, His chosen ones. The poured-out wine represented His blood, spilled out for us—His vow to give up His very life for His bride. That's God's model for covenant love. And when we choose to enter into covenant with Christ, we freely offer all we are to Him, just as He has freely offered Himself for us. Every time we take communion, we remember our covenant relationship with the King of all kings. We are saying in essence, "My blood is yours to spill, my body is yours to break."

Christ is our model for covenant love. The covenant we make with our spouse on our wedding day is a small reflection of the covenant Christ has made with us. On your wedding day, remember your covenant with Christ by taking communion together as a couple. Allow the broken bread and poured-out wine to illustrate the covenant you are making with each other, a sacred vow to give all you have and all you are to your spouse for a lifetime, a choice to lay down even your life for your marriage partner, just as Christ laid down His life for you. Remember that from this day, you are no longer your own—you are in holy covenant with your spouse, and your two lives have become one...forever.

The Greatest Lover of All Time

How should you love your spouse? Just as Christ loves His bride. Selflessly. Sacrificially. Unconditionally. To love as Christ loves is humanly impossible; His version of love is out of our reach. But when we enter into covenant with Christ, He makes His heavenly version of love available by demonstrating it in and through our lives. So we too can love like the greatest Lover of all time.

Princely honor set aside
As He washed the feet of His humble bride
Pouring out His breath and blood
As a sacrifice for the one He loved

And this love that spills out everything
Is the love I pledge to you
Like the One who gave it all for me
I will give my life for you

CHORUS
All I have, all I am
I give to you in covenant
Like broken bread and poured-out wine
I'll love you like
The greatest Lover of all time

Heroic love that led a King
To choose the road of suffering
Selflessness that just begins
Where human understanding ends

And this love that takes the lowest place
Is the love that I now choose
Like the One who gave His life away
I will give my life for you

His love gave without holding back
So I will love you like that
His love paid the ultimate price
So I will lay down my life

CHAPTER THREE

A Lasting Kiss

Beyond the Touch of Human Lips

*Explore the boundless depths
of lifelong intimacy.*

*Hollywood would have us believe that physical
beauty and sexual performance in the bedroom
are the key ingredients to a marriage that thrives.
However, it's not "head turners" who make their
spouses happy for a lifetime but rather those
who learn how to turn a heart. And "heart
turning" is something anyone can learn to do.*

ou may *now* kiss the bride!"

What an odd statement to throw into a wedding ceremony! Why give a couple the permission to kiss on their wedding day, when they've most likely already exchanged saliva a thousand times?

That traditional verbiage seems strange to most contemporary couples. We live in a world where intimate kisses have lost their sacred essence. In some relationships a kiss is carelessly given away only hours into the shallow affair. In others, a kiss is treated as a mere formality of expressing romantic interest. No wonder we've lost an understanding of saving the sacred touches, the kisses and the caresses, for the perfect God-orchestrated moments.

The root of this seemingly strange tradition of "*now* kissing the bride" grows out of a forgotten paradigm of sexual intimacy and physical touch prior to marriage. It's an ancient understanding of physical touch—one that reserved all sexual expressions of affection for the wedding day and beyond. So when a groom was "allowed" to kiss his bride, it actually meant that the time had come for him to kiss her *for the very first time.*

Saving physical intimacy is actually based on a principle of God's kingdom. Jesus once said to His disciples, "Do not give dogs what is sacred; do not throw your pearls to pigs" (Matthew 7:6).

Dogs and pigs have no sense of value. A dog, for instance, will happily befoul the foot of da Vinci's famous statue of David just as naturally as he would a fire hydrant. And a pig will snarf down a pearl just as fast as he would gobble down a stone pebble mixed in the mud. Dogs and pigs can't be trusted with anything of value.

God teaches us to entrust things of value in our life only to those who have first proven that they are worthy of such a trust.

And of all the things of great value in our life, one of the most precious is our sexual essence. It's the equivalent of the holy of holies in God's temple in Jerusalem. It's the set-apart place of our beings, and beyond the presence of God, it is reserved for only one person to ever access.

God has already defined who we can allow to enter this sacred sanctuary of our being. It's one who has proven that they will value it and protect its sacredness as their most prized possession—one willing to give up everything in covenant as proof of their sincerity, proof of their intentions.

Leslie and I aren't saying that saving kisses for your wedding day is a requirement to lasting love, but we *are* advocates of allowing God to be the director of the progression of sacred touches in your relationship. A sensual kiss, when orchestrated by God Himself, is a statement of covenant intent. It should hold deep meaning and significance and not simply be a catalyst for sensual stimulation. When God sets the stage for a kiss, a kiss never loses its beauty...*ever.*

The Risk of Intimacy

God intends a wedding day to be the Christmas morning of a couple's romance. It's the day the sacred gifts are given as a means of celebrating the newly born covenant bond.

A couple can experience a certain dimension of intimacy prior to their wedding day, but God intends intimacy to blossom into a riot of springtime color on and beyond a wedding day. It's the day you bare yourself, body and soul. It's the day of extreme vulnerability...total nakedness. It's the day when the sacred threshold is finally crossed, when the veil is parted, opening up a way for our lover to enter our most holy and set-apart places.

Intimacy has a simple formula—total trust and total acceptance. A Christ-centered marriage has no place for performing or acting—everything is genuine, everything is real. And in this authentic context, God desires for us to share our most precious and most sacred pearls—our deepest feelings, the passionate and sometimes crazy desires of our heart, and the greatest struggles and fears swirling within our souls. It's being undressed—and therefore, helpless before our lover's inspecting gaze.

When we hand over the most sacred possessions of our soul, we make ourselves vulnerable. For instance, our lover may laugh, jeer, mock, sneer, or even reject us when we bare our all. Such is the risk of intimacy. Those who want to reach the highest heights of heavenly love must must all face this risk. For in the face of such a vulnerability, when instead of rejecting us, our lover embraces and accepts us, we experience the closest brush with the unmerited and unconditional love of God our souls may ever feel this side of heaven. When instead of hurting us, our lover adores our every little idiosyncrasy, the result is a burgeoning intimacy, a closeness of heavenly proportions.

A kiss is a physical representation of what marriage is and what a wedding day opens up for a lifetime to follow. It is the sharing of our most delicate, most sensitive sexual essence, the becoming one without distance between, without thought of self, with only the giving of affection, the spilling out of ourselves 'til death parts us.

"Do not give dogs what is sacred; do not throw your pearls to pigs."

It's very easy to be dog-like and piggish in our relationships and not hold sacred the vulnerability of our lover. Marriage is the context God designed for lovers to take the risk of intimacy, but few modern couples have been taught what to do with these sacred possessions. We may correct our spouses when they share their fears, we may let out a slight chuckle when they impart to us their dreams, and we may even criticize them as they bare themselves naked before us. In other words, we can easily take their vulnerability and instead of guarding it, snub it and wound them deeply.

That's why a wedding day is such an important training ground. If a couple learns to guard and preserve the sacred elements of their physical relationship prior to marriage, they already have a foundation upon which to build for success after they exchange vows and in the years to come.

Marriage intimacy can grow only in the soil of constant guardedness—tended by total trust and total acceptance. It can grow only when the secrecy of the couple's sanctuary life is protected like the vault at Fort Knox. What takes place within the bedroom *stays* in the bedroom, and what is shared in confidence *stays* in confidence. That is Marriage Intimacy 101: Preserve the sacred before the wedding day, and then preserve it with all the pluck of a valiant warrior forever after.

A kiss may not seem like much within our culture nowadays, but in God's perspective a sensual kiss is an extremely sacred symbol of covenant. A kiss on a wedding day can quickly be forgotten by those who treat it as mere tradition. But to those who give it the respect it deserves and cherish it as the expression of their total surrender, it can become a tender and profoundly meaningful reminder of a couple's love. Every time your lips meet, you are saying to your spouse, "You are my chosen one!"

PUTTING A LASTING KISS INTO ACTION ON YOUR WEDDING DAY

Before the Wedding:
Protecting Sacred Things

$\mathcal{I}$n our past relationships, Leslie and I had lost the sacred beauty of a kiss. We had thrown this beautiful expression of love away carelessly in short-term flings. So when God wrote our love story, we wanted a kiss to regain its luster, its sacredness. We decided to save our first kiss until our wedding ceremony. It wasn't an easy commitment to keep! But at the moment the pastor said, "You may now kiss your bride!" and our lips met for the first time, we knew it was worth it. Still to this day, a kiss has never lost its beauty between us. It is a sacred expression of our covenant commitment to each other.

Saving your first kiss until your wedding is by no means a requirement for a God-scripted love story. But protecting the sacred things *is* a necessary ingredient for romance from heaven. Even if you've already exchanged many kisses and caresses with your spouse-to-be, start protecting the sacred things today. Being set apart sexually doesn't mean merely saving *technical* virginity until your wedding day; rather, it means honoring each other by guarding physical forms of expression until your covenant has been established. Prayerfully make a commitment together to protect the physical side of your relationship, and discuss specifically what that will mean for you before your wedding day.

(Having teammates in your life to keep you accountable to your commitment is a huge benefit.) When you treat each and every form of sensual expression as a sacred gift not to be taken lightly, you will experience the amazing beauty of a lasting kiss.

After the Wedding:
Savoring True Intimacy

If you have waited for your wedding night to explore the fullness of sexual intimacy, you are most likely far more excited about the honeymoon than the wedding ceremony! But as wonderful as sexual closeness can be, intimacy includes much more than physical touch. One of my favorite things in my marriage with Leslie is simply lying in bed together at night and just holding her. That may sound unexciting, but there is more to it than just having a warm body next to me. Leslie and I love just *being* together. We share life at the deepest level. We know the good and the bad about each other, and still we accept each other completely. Even with no words, we understand each other better than anyone else on earth. That's the beauty of true intimacy. And because we share such a depth of closeness, the physical side of our relationship is all the more amazing.

On your honeymoon, remember that true intimacy, not just sexual closeness, is the ultimate goal. Be sure to texture your kisses and caresses with plenty of talking, listening, and exploring the depths of who your spouse is. Get your marriage off to the right start by savoring true intimacy from day one.

Dreams

Some things are too beautiful to be expressed in words. Marriage intimacy designed by God is one of those things. May this wordless song help capture, if only on a small level, the sparkling wonder of shared love. The Author of romance is always the One holding the pen when dreams come true.

CHAPTER FOUR

A Cheering Witness
Beyond the Gifts and Guest Book

*Embrace the loving support of
God-given teammates.*

*A wedding party shouldn't be chosen merely out
of social obligation but out of a desire to surround
yourself with a community that can hold you
accountable to your sacred covenant vows.*

lot of humans live on this earth, and not all of them are going to be cheering us down the aisle. Not many of them are going to be willing to travel great distances, rent a tux, buy a pink puffed-sleeved bridesmaid's dress, and stand next to us hoping not to faint as we exchange vows with our life-long lover. The frank and honest truth is that 99.9 percent of this planet's population probably doesn't even realize that we exist, let alone that we are getting married.

But don't despair. A few of those countless human beings swarming the earth's surface *do* care, *are* excited, and *will* drive four thousand miles round trip in their rickety 1987 Chevy pickup to make sure that they are there for us.

We all have our "few." And these few can help to bring out an additional God-colored luster in our wedding day.

Friend of the Bridegroom

For those who are familiar with the story of Jesus, the name John the Baptist will certainly ring a bell. The Bible refers to him as the forerunner to the ministry of Christ. In other words, he set the stage and prepared everything so that all eyes could see Jesus when the time was right.

Another name the Scriptures use to describe John the Baptist is "friend of the bridegroom" (John 3:29 NASB), which was the equivalent term in the Hebrew culture for what we know as the best man. That's right! John the Baptist was, in a sense, Jesus' best man.

Unfortunately, over the past two thousand years, much of the significance of that sacred position has been lost. The erosion of the concept has taken many years to fully manifest, but now a best man no longer holds a sacred position of intimate trust. Now the best man's role is usually just a casual and often crude position of dudehood.

Best men today throw bachelor parties and are responsible for the wedding ring, the practical jokes, and the car decoration before the bride and groom depart off into the sunset. However, best men in God's economy are not casual jokesters but rather men devoted to God and willing to give up their life to preserve a friend in covenant.

God appointed John the Baptist to care for His bride (God's set-apart people) and prepare her for the arrival of her Groom (Jesus Christ). In the Hebrew culture, this concept made complete sense. The Jewish custom was for a man to entrust his bride-to-be into the care of his most trusted friend while he went off and prepared a home for himself and his future wife. While the groom was gone, the friend of the bridegroom was responsible for protecting the purity of his friend's fiancé. He guarded her and made sure that nothing would hinder her in her relationship with her future groom. And when the groom finally returned to claim his bride, the friend of the bridegroom would decrease in the bride's life so that the bridegroom could increase and take his rightful position.

So when John the Baptist said the words, "He [Jesus] must increase, but I must decrease" (John 3:30 NASB), he was using terminology that a Jew would understand in the context of a wedding covenant.

Jesus said that "Among those born of women there has not risen anyone greater than John the Baptist" (Matthew 11:11). Jesus didn't just pick any old Joe Shmoe to hold that sacred position in his life. He picked the most excellent of men.

On our wedding day, it is important that we gain Christlike discrimination toward those we are choosing to stand beside us. Remember, on a wedding day, we are entering into a sacred covenant bond that is irrevocable and lifelong. This isn't something to take lightly. We do well to surround ourselves with others that take it just as seriously as we do.

The Cheering Witness

A wedding ceremony is not merely two people covenanting before God—it is two people covenanting before God *and* before a select host of witnesses. It includes a wedding party covenanting before God to serve this covenant bond and help preserve its sacred wholeness for as long as both shall live.

If God Himself picked out a friend for the enactment of His covenant with mankind, let's follow His example and pick the most excellent of men and women to assist us in the enactment of covenant on our sacred day.

A wedding covenant is a sacred bond not only between husband and wife but also between husband, wife, and friends. They don't all share the same kind of covenant, but the friends' commitment is just as valid and grandly important to the long-term success of the couple's marriage.

Grasping the Deeper Meaning

Most of us read about John the Baptist in the Bible and find his story interesting, but then we move on through the text, never realizing the amazing applicability of his example to our marriages. John the Baptist is one of the most profound pictures of what God designed marriage to be. God asks each of us, as a spouse, to be a "friend of the bridegroom"—to be a forerunner in our spouse's life to prepare the way for them to understand and apprehend Christ in all His fullness and glory.

Contrary to our typical way of thinking, marriage isn't only about two people in love vowing to live in faithfulness 'til death parts them. Marriage is about two people serving each other, preparing each other for a *heavenly* Spouse, the ultimate Bridegroom, Jesus Christ.

Marriage presents a constant choice to decrease so that Christ may increase in your spouse's life. Long and short, marriage is about Christ—more and more and more of Christ every day for an entire life. When both spouses choose to befriend the heavenly Bridegroom, the natural result is a romantic and poetic love for all time. Purity and faithfulness are the results of the daily decreasing of self's agenda and the fanning into flame of the heavenly Bridegroom's agenda.

A wedding day demonstrates this profound reality—this magnificent truth. A wedding is about a poetic love, a sacred vow, and a lasting kiss, but it is also about those willing to befriend the bride and groom through a covenant of lifelong service.

PUTTING A CHEERING WITNESS INTO ACTION ON YOUR WEDDING DAY

Choosing Your Witnesses

$\mathcal{I}$t's very probable that the friends you pick as your best man and maid of honor will not fully understand the divine significance of their roles. They may not realize that by standing with you and being witnesses to your marriage covenant, they are agreeing to the sacred responsibility of holding you to that covenant. So take some time to explain it to them. Tell them how highly you value their position in your life. Ask them to join with you in witnessing your covenant commitment to your spouse, and then invite them to hold you accountable to your vow from this day forward.

Asking your friends to stand with you in your wedding ceremony is to bestow a tremendous honor on them, but they will sense an even greater privilege when they realize how truly significant their role is. To be a friend of the bridegroom is a sacred position, a position both of honor and great responsibility.

Honoring Friends and Family

The joys of a wedding celebration aren't just for you and your spouse-to-be. They are also for the people who have invested in your life throughout the years, those who have helped you come to the altar and take the sacred vows. A wedding day is the perfect time to express honor and appreciation for those who have empowered you to become the person you are, those who gave you life, love, and unwavering support—your cheering witnesses.

Think of creative ways to honor these people on your wedding day. For example, use the wedding program to write a memorable note to your parents, siblings, and close friends, thanking them for all they have done for you. Or dedicate a special song to them at the reception or during the ceremony. Consider writing your parents (or other significant people) a heartfelt letter expressing your gratitude for all they have given you, and giving it to them on your wedding day—it will be a lifelong treasure. Regardless of the means you choose, make sure you go out of your way to honor those who have invested in your life. Make this a day that your cheering witnesses will never forget.

More of Him

As Leslie's earthly lover, my goal is not to draw her to myself but to lead her closer to her true Bridegroom, Jesus Christ, through my love. Like John the Baptist, my job is to decrease so that Christ might increase in her life. And the beauty of a Christ-centered marriage is that as both individuals grow closer to Jesus Christ, they naturally grow closer to each other.

I stand before you now
With a sacred vow
To love you for a lifetime
To give you all my heart

But there's One who's there
Where my love will fail
And He is all that I'm not

So now I must decrease
Usher His full glory in
May there be less of me and more of Him

CHORUS
When you see me
May you see reflections
Of One who's perfection won't end

When you hold me
May you feel the touch of
The One who loves much more
Than I can comprehend

When you fall more
In love with me
May you fall more in love with Him

As the years go by
May I always try
To draw you closer to your one true destiny

My love for you is great
But it's just a taste
Of what's waiting in eternity

So now I must decrease
Usher His full glory in
May there be less of me and more of Him

CHAPTER FIVE

A New Beginning
Beyond "Happily Ever After"

*Enter into a Christ-built adventure
that has only just begun.*

*Often the first weeks of newly wedded wonder are
the most enjoyable of the entire marriage. This
shouldn't be the case. In God's design, marriage
only gets sweeter with time. Though it is amazing
now, the best days are always still to come.*

Christ performed His first miracle on earth while attending a wedding.

Why choose a wedding for such a momentous occasion? Because a wedding is the perfect enunciation of His great plan. It's a picture of selfless love, binding covenant, sacred generosity, and sacrificial friendship. A wedding is an earthly picture of God's heavenly agenda. God came to earth to rescue His bride. He came to earth for the purpose of covenanting with the ones He loved.

As far as God is concerned, a wedding isn't merely a formality; it is a demonstration of His gospel to all those who witness on earth and in the heavenly realms.

Christ chose a profoundly beautiful miracle to be His first one. It wasn't something glamorous like raising the dead or giving sight to a blind man. In fact, on the surface His very first miracle seems rather anticlimactic. Many of us often write off His first miracle as something He did to warm up for the bigger things to come. But God was making a statement with His first miracle—a statement that none of us should miss.

As the story goes, during the latter stages of this wedding celebration, Mary told Jesus that the wine was running out. In a Hebrew wedding this was tantamount to disaster. Jesus asked the servants to fill six enormous stone jars standing nearby with water, and then he told them to draw some out and take it to the master of the banquet.

When the master of the banquet tasted what was in the cup, he didn't taste water, but wine. He called the bridegroom aside and said, "Everyone brings out the choice wine first and then the cheaper wine after the guests have had too much to drink; but you have saved the best till now" (John 2:10).

The model of the world's love brings out the choice wine in the beginning of the celebration, and then from that point on the quality disintegrates. So often young lovers find an electric sensual love in the beginning of their affair only to whittle it down into a passionless bore as the weeks and months pass. But Christ has a different model, a revolutionary model, which He proved with His very first miracle.

The quality of the celebration, the romance, and the intimacy only get *better* with time *when we invite Him to the wedding and allow Him to build the marriage*.

When Christ isn't invited to the wedding, the six stone jars remain unused, and no miracle takes place. The sweet wine is used up in the beginning of the romance, and the stone jars are unable to fill themselves full of water and transform it into a fine wine.

The difference between a failed wedding and a successful one comes down to one very simple thing—the guest list. Was Christ invited?

If not, the marriage may start out with song and dance, but it ends with disappointment and regret. The wine will run out.

Every day around this world, stone jars remain empty and the spark of celebratory love fades with the turn of the hour hand on the clock. Christ was not invited to the wedding; He was not asked to fill our stone jars with the ordinary substance of life and transform it into the extraordinary substance of lifelong and ever-growing marital beauty.

When He is our Guest of Honor, our Wedding Coordinator, the Testator of our covenant, not only will our celebratory wine never run out, but it will get tastier and tastier as the love story progresses.

This is God's way. He invented married love to be a foretaste of *His* love. He designed marriage to be an earthly sampling of eternal life in heaven with Him as our Bridegroom. And His version of love, just like fine wine, gets better and better as time passes.

Our wedding day is not only an opportunity to display these amazing truths of God's kingdom, but it is also only the first of a million more opportunities in marriage to showcase the glory of God for this world to see and comprehend His nature.

On your wedding day, we encourage you to set out your life, like the six stone jars, before Christ. Ask Him to fill you full of Himself, the Living Water, and transform your relationship into a miracle that proves that poetic love only gets sweeter and sweeter with the passing of time.

PUTTING A NEW BEGINNING INTO
ACTION ON YOUR WEDDING DAY

A Prayer of Dedication

Consider inviting the spiritual leaders in your life to partici-
pate in a time of prayer in your wedding ceremony—agreeing
with you as you dedicate your marriage fully to Jesus Christ.
Leslie and I invited eight of our spiritual "fathers" to gather
around us during our wedding to pray for our new life together. They offered prayers for our future ministry, future
children, and future decisions—we prayed that God would
always remain the Author of our love story. Joining with our
cheering witnesses in consecrating our marriage to Christ
was an unforgettable part of our wedding day.

We also invited our parents and grandparents to pray for
our marriage during the ceremony—they had left a legacy
of love and faithfulness that we wanted to honor. Their
prayers that day were beautiful and meaningful.

Including so much prayer in a wedding ceremony might
sound boring or unromantic, but it was actually one of
the most significant things about our wedding day. By surrounding our new union with heartfelt prayer, we made
Christ the Guest of Honor. We remembered that this day
was not ultimately about Eric and Leslie...it was about
Christ's amazing love and faithfulness to us, His chosen
ones, His bride.

Even if you don't have parents or a large group of spiritual leaders who can offer heartfelt prayers during your

wedding ceremony, you can still make Christ the Guest of Honor on your wedding day. Pray together as a couple, asking for Christ to come and turn your ordinary lives into an extraordinary display of His love and grace. Marriage is the most challenging and incredible adventure you will ever embark upon—and unless you are leaning on the arm of your true Bridegroom, you will not have the strength to go the distance. Remember that He honors those who honor Him.

This Love

Can we be sure our love will last? Yes, if our love is of the heavenly, not earthly, variety. When we build our marriage upon Christ's love, He transforms our ordinary human romance into an extraordinary supernatural display of His forever kind of love…He fills our water jars with the choicest of wines.

I've heard it said that love fades
Like thirsty flowers in the sun
They say romance is like the summer rain
That melts away as quickly as it comes

But what do they know of a love that's built upon
More than the shifting sand of earthly fairy tales
My love for you will only grow from this day on
This love will thrive where others falter and grow stale

This love will stand where others fail

CHORUS
This love is made of more than promises alone
This love is fueled by heaven's strength and not our own
Beyond roses and diamond rings
Beyond the temporary things
That human plans and human dreams are made of
Angels sing of the wonder of this love

I know that there'll be hard times
When we're torn and beaten by the wind
But when clear perspective is hard to find
That's when His supernatural sight begins

We will see the power of a love that only grows
More beautiful by all the handiwork of time
Through the trials what we have will become more valuable
If we will let Him turn our water into wine

This love will last for all time

Epilogue

Beautiful love stories don't happen
accidentally. They happen on purpose.

mid all the wreckage of failed modern marriages, a new generation of young lovers still believes marriage can be something magical and lifelong. To all you young idealists who still maintain this "happily ever after" vision, we raise our glasses in admiration. You are the hope of the future. Modern marriage teeters uncomfortably on the precipice of ruin. We need marriages that once again showcase the beauty of heaven on earth.

A wedding day is just the beginning of one of the most extraordinary adventures. But few, when they arrive at the altar, are prepared to tackle such an extreme challenge. They arrive at the foot of this massive Everest with a dozen roses and a diamond ring and hope that will be enough to help them reach the highest heights.

An amazing marriage *is* possible for anyone willing to do whatever it takes to attain it. Many want a lifelong love story, but few are willing to relinquish their selfish agenda in order to actually find it. Our hope is that you will choose to be one of the few who are willing to venture down the path of selflessness and lifelong poetic love. For when you allow Jesus Christ to script your love story, your romance and fulfillment will have no end. A love story built in heaven is not a romance without trials and challenges. But the trials and challenges can strengthen the covenant you establish on your wedding day.

A wedding day is only one day. But it's a day unlike any other in our life. To experience the fullness of what God intended marriage to be, we must not enter into this sacred covenant lightly but with great intentionality and reverence. We must place Christ at the top of our guest list and make this holy day a celebration of His love for us.

Whatever happened to "happily ever after"? It is waiting to be rediscovered. We invite you to be among those who find it once again. We invite you to prove wrong all the naysayers who believe that marital bliss erodes with time. We invite you to let God script your wedding day and your marriage through good times and bad, in sickness and in health, for richer or for poorer, through the challenges and the joys life brings. Then it will truly be said of your love...*and they lived happily ever after.*

Other Good Harvest House Reading

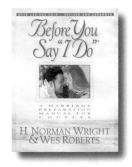

BEFORE YOU SAY "I DO"
H. Norman Wright

Explore how to clarify role expectations, establish healthy sexual relationship, handle finances, and acquire a solid understanding of how to develop a biblical relationship. More than 500,000 copies sold.

HOW CAN I BE SURE?
Bob Phillips

For more than 20 years this pre-marriage inventory has helped couples contemplating marriage. As a couple, you will explore your thoughts and feelings, find areas of agreement, and develop a basis for resolving disagreements.

JUST MARRIED
Margaret Feinberg

This book will engagingly walk you through your first years of marriage and tackle one of the biggest challenges for newlyweds—establishing your relationships with God both as individuals and as a married couple.

HARVEST HOUSE
PUBLISHERS